.

The

Interview

Coach

A Guide for Successful Job Interviews
and
Answers to 66 Interview Questions

Lorna Hegarty

www.coachlorna.com
lorna@coachlorna.com

ISBN: 978-1-988317-03-8

Published by LCH Resources Limited

First Edition - June 2016

Disclaimer:

The advice, recommendations, descriptions and the methods described in this book are presented solely for educational purposes, and the author assumes no liability whatsoever for any loss or damage that results from the use of any material in this book. Some names and identifying details have been changed to protect the privacy of individuals.

Other books by Lorna Hegarty:

The Wealthy Teen – A Guide for Teens, Parents & Mentors
The Seven Essential Practices of Great Leaders
Parenting IS Leadership

Congratulations on your purchase of **The Interview Coach – A Guide for a Successful Job Interviews, and Answers to 66 Interview Questions**. By acquiring this book, you will have simple, but effective techniques to use in your next interview.

There are many job search books on the market. Based on feedback, this book gives you space to record your answer to each question. The space follows directly after the question, and the explanation as to what the interviewer is looking for. This book helps you work through the process of developing the best answer for YOU to give. So, in your next interview, you will be better able to understand what the interviewer is looking for, and be more prepared to sell yourself.

Having completed this book, you will know *how* and *what* to prepare.

Remember – the only time you'll ever see "success" before "work" is in the dictionary!

L Hegarty

Lorna Hegarty

Contents

Instructions

1. Work through the exercises in the book. Begin to formulate your own answers, depending on your own interview situation, your strengths and skills and experience.

2. Once you have written out your answers to the questions begin by reading them and re-reading them, until they sound perfect and you are comfortable with the responses you have written.

3. As you gain confidence, sit in front of a mirror and look at yourself as you give your answers out loud, reading them from your workbook – watch your facial expressions, your body language, hand movements, etc.

4. As you get even more comfortable with the above steps, record your answers onto a voice recorder so that you can play your answers out loud later. Listen more often as your interview day gets closer.

5. For those that want to be "pros" in the interview game – videotape yourself talking through the answers – you will be surprised what you will learn! It may seem scary, but it is the fastest way to pick up on improvements you can make.

You don't have to be scheduled for an interview for these steps to be useful. If you want to brush up on your skills, or do some advance planning, you will still get the benefit from this exercise. Answers will be written down for you to review when the time comes. Don't forget there isn't always lots of advance warning before an interview. You may only get a day or two to prepare, so the more you can do in advance, the more prepared you will be.

Part I – Strengths or Attributes

What ten personal attributes do you have, which would be useful in the job, for which you are being interviewed? (Place a check mark beside those that apply, then write 10 of them that would be important for the job you are being interviewed for, on the list that follows.)

Some ideas:

- Accurate
- Adaptable
- Ambitious
- Analytical
- Approachable
- Articulate
- Assertive
- Autonomous
- Calm
- Capable
- Careful
- Cautious
- Committed
- Communicative
- Competitive
- Compassionate
- Competent
- Conceptual
- Confident
- Conscientious
- Consensus builder
- Consistent
- Conventional
- Cool-headed
- Cooperative
- Creative
- Critical
- Curious
- Daring
- Decisive
- Dedicated
- Dependable
- Determined
- Diligent
- Direct
- Disciplined
- Discreet
- Easy-going
- Efficient
- Empathetic
- Energetic
- Enthusiastic
- Entrepreneurial
- Experienced
- Flexible
- Forthright
- Forward thinking
- Friendly
- Hard-working
- Honest
- Imaginative
- Initiative
- Knowledgeable
- Leadership

- Loyal
- Methodical
- Meticulous
- Objective
- Observant
- Open-minded
- Organized
- Patient
- Perceptive
- Perfectionist
- Persistent
- Persuasive
- Physically fit
- Positive
- Productive
- Proficient
- Practical
- Precise
- Punctual
- Relationship builder
- Reliable
- Results-oriented
- Responsible
- Resourceful
- Self-confident
- Self-disciplined
- Sense of humor
- Sensitive
- Service-oriented
- Tactful
- Systematic
- Team worker
- Team builder
- Thorough
- Thoughtful
- Trustworthy
- Understanding

1. _____

2. _____

3. _____

4. _____

5. _____

6. _____

7. _____

8. _____

9. _____

10. _____

Personal strengths or attributes are the foundation of your personality.

Job-related or Transferable Skills

What ten strengths (i.e. ability to use technology, etc.) do you have which would be useful in the job for which you are being interviewed? (Place a check mark beside those that apply, then write 10 of them that would be important for the job you are being interviewed for, on the list that follows.)

Some ideas:

- Accounting
- Administration
- Advising
- Analyzing
- Artistic
- Assembling
- Budgeting
- Calculating
- Clarifying
- Classifying
- Coaching
- Comparing
- Compiling
- Communicating
- Consulting
- Convincing
- Coordinating
- Counseling
- Deciding
- Defining
- Delegating
- Designing
- Determining outcomes
- Displaying
- Drawing
- Driving
- Editing
- Estimating
- Evaluating
- Financing
- Following
- Generating Solutions
- Helping
- Illustrating
- Inspecting
- Instructing
- Interpreting
- Interviewing
- Investigating
- Keyboarding
- Languages
- Listening
- Managing
- Mechanical
- Mentoring
- Monitoring
- Motivating
- Negotiating
- Networking
- Numbers
- Observing
- Operating
- Organizing
- Persuading
- Planning
- Presenting

- Programming
- Promoting
- Public Contact
- Public Relations
- Public Speaking
- Purchasing
- Reading
- Recording
- Repairing
- Reporting
- Researching
- Responding
- Scheduling
- Selling
- Serving
- Setting up
- Speaking
- Studying
- Supervising
- Teaching
- Team Work
- Technical drawing
- Testing ideas
- Tools
- Translating
- Troubleshooting
- Updating
- Writing reports

1. _____

2. _____

3. _____

4. _____

5. _____

6. _____

7. _____

8. _____

9. _____

10. _____

Job-related or Transferable Skills are learned skills that you can transfer to a new job.

Part II - Behavioral Interview Technique

Before you go for your job interview, it will be helpful for you to know that Behavioral Interview questions are a major part of most job interviews. Employers and hiring managers use these types of questions in order to get an idea of whether or not you have the skills and competencies that are needed for the job.

The rationale for using this technique is that if they know how you performed in the past, it will help give a sense of **how you might do in the future.**

For you as the candidate, you'll need to prepare answers *(basically "interview stories")* that highlight the different strengths, attributes, competencies, and skillsets the employer is looking for. Most candidates have a general idea of how to answer these questions, however, the answers usually are too long and unfocused, and won't put a candidate in the best light.

That's why you'll need to make a **concerted effort** to create these stories and adapt them to the **relevant competencies.**

How to Answer Behavioral Interview Questions?

The best way to answer a behavioural interview question is to formulate a CAR Story

CAR Stories

Look at the 20 strengths you listed in Part I.

Using any 10 of those strengths, think about stories or situations that would support your claims of having those strengths. In the interview you must be able to back up each strength with a real live situation of when you used it. To help you do this, become familiar with the concept of **CAR** stories which will give you a frame to work within. You will be organized and know exactly what important details you need to include and emphasize in your story.

C ... stands for the *challenge* you were faced with:

- What were you tasked to do?

A ... is the *action* you decided to take:

- Include why you chose that action.

R ... reminds you to talk about the *results*:

- Use some form of measurement if appropriate – did you save time or money?
- What feedback did you get from others on how you did?

Make sure your story is concise and clear and covers all the areas in the **CAR** stories.

This can be the receptionist who goes the extra mile by gathering information for a frustrated caller – although she or he did not have to. It could be the creative manager who started a reward system for his or her employees; it could be the mechanic who checked a few additional parts of the car with no extra charge. Perhaps the customer focused bank teller who brought a chair for an elderly customer to rest on, it could be designing a computer system to handle statistics in a way nobody had thought about.

*Formulate your CAR stories below. You can start by using bullet points and be sure to cover the **Challenge** – **Approach** and **Results**.*

Take as many of the strengths or attributes as well as job related or transferable skills that you listed on pages 9 and 10, and pages 11 and 12 to build your CAR stories around. Following is space for you to develop 10 CAR stories, as they relate to the position you are being interviewed for.

What Strength / Attribute or Job Related / Transferable Skill Is Being Addressed? _____ Generating Solutions

Challenge *(EXAMPLE)*

I was working in an industrial factory where Health and Safety was very important. When visitors from Head Office would come to the plant, we had to do a 15-minute safety briefing with them. I was not always available to do the safety briefing and I noticed sometimes it only took others a few minutes to do their briefing.

Action *(EXAMPLE)*

I wanted to make sure everybody got a full safety briefing no matter who was conducting it. I developed a one-page form that both the employee and the guest reviewed and signed before entering the plant.

Results *(EXAMPLE)*

Now every person who enters the building is given consistent safety awareness training which puts us in compliance with all of our safety policies and procedures. We scan and file all of the documents in case they are needed. After the first month, my safety form had been adopted throughout all the plants in our company, and I was nominated for a Safety Award.

1. What Strength / Attribute or Job Related / Transferable Skill Is Being Addressed? _____

Challenge

_____

_____

_____

_____

_____

Action

_____

_____

_____

_____

_____

Results

_____

_____

_____

_____

_____

2. What Strength / Attribute or Job Related / Transferable Skill Is Being Addressed? _____

Challenge

_____

_____

_____

_____

_____

Action

_____

_____

_____

_____

_____

Results

_____

_____

_____

_____

_____

3. What Strength / Attribute or Job Related / Transferable
   Skill Is Being Addressed? _____

Challenge

_____

_____

_____

_____

_____

Action

_____

_____

_____

_____

_____

Results

_____

_____

_____

_____

_____

4. What Strength / Attribute or Job Related / Transferable Skill Is Being Addressed? _____

Challenge

_____

_____

_____

_____

_____

Action

_____

_____

_____

_____

_____

Results

_____

_____

_____

_____

5. What Strength / Attribute or Job Related / Transferable Skill Is Being Addressed? _____

Challenge

_____

_____

_____

_____

_____

Action

_____

_____

_____

_____

_____

Results

_____

_____

_____

_____

_____

6. What Strength / Attribute or Job Related / Transferable Skill Is Being Addressed? _____

Challenge

_____

_____

_____

_____

_____

Action

_____

_____

_____

_____

_____

Results

_____

_____

_____

_____

_____

7. What Strength / Attribute or Job Related / Transferable Skill Is Being Addressed? _____

Challenge

_____

_____

_____

_____

_____

Action

_____

_____

_____

_____

_____

Results

_____

_____

_____

_____

_____

8. What Strength / Attribute or Job Related / Transferable Skill Is Being Addressed? _____

Challenge

_____

_____

_____

_____

_____

Action

_____

_____

_____

_____

_____

Results

_____

_____

_____

_____

_____

9. What Strength / Attribute or Job Related / Transferable Skill Is Being Addressed? _____

Challenge

_____
_____
_____
_____
_____

Action

_____
_____
_____
_____
_____

Results

_____
_____
_____
_____
_____

10. What Strength / Attribute or Job Related / Transferable Skill Is Being Addressed? _____

Challenge

_____
_____
_____
_____
_____

Action

_____
_____
_____
_____
_____

Results

_____
_____
_____
_____
_____

Part III – Interview Questions

The interview is a great chance to show who you are, and why you are an ideal candidate for the job. You should always go into any interview with basic understanding of what the job is, what attributes would best suit the job, and match them to your qualifications and experience. What follows are some of the many interview questions you will come across when being interviewed. No single interview will ask all of these questions, however, these are a good guide to get you thinking about how to present yourself in the interview. One of the key things employers want to evaluate in the interview is to ask how you have responded in situations that this job may require of you. It is always a great idea to use the format of CARS (Challenge, Action, Results) for any situation. In advance, think of what skill and attribute matches you have with the job you are being interviewed for and how you can best let the interviewer know that you would be the right person to select.

Some of these questions will be easy to answer, and some more difficult. By practicing answers before an interview, you will have less chance of a surprise question that takes you off balance, when you have done a general preparation. Remember to always keep your answers relevant to the job you are applying for.

Keep in mind – if you were the employer, what would you want to know before you hired someone? **The following** questions are ones that I have asked an applicant or heard others ask in an interview.

- Use your judgment for the answers. If you are in a line of work that my suggested answer doesn't make sense for, please adjust accordingly.

- It is ok to take a 'cheat sheet' with you to the interview. You can take a list of a few of your CAR stories – the titles of the CAR stories, so you can take a quick glance at them at the interview if you draw a blank. They are not to be read from, just a memory jogger. Best if typed out neatly and only brought out if you get stuck on a question.

- Sometimes one word responses are requested for answers. Simply respond, and then you could ask the interviewer if they would like an example of why you responded that way. Not every single answer *has* to be a CAR story.

- Remember – the interviewer wants to know you are able to do the job – and that you are the type of person they are looking for.

- Be selective in what you say. Always promote the positive things about you, and be honest.

- When you are in the interview speak with enthusiasm and conviction and be friendly.

Now, on to the interview. Let's Go!

1. Tell me about yourself.

This question is an ice-breaker. It is meant to give you a chance to tell a little about yourself. While this is an opportunity to get to know you a little bit, most interviewers don't want to know how many cats you own, or about your gardening skills unless this relates directly to the job. Speak about your professional life, and relate what you can to the job you are being interviewed for. Your resume is a snapshot of your professional life, but they won't get a full picture from it, and may not have looked at it since you were picked for the interview.

_____

_____

_____

_____

_____

_____

_____

_____

_____

_____

_____

_____

_____

2. What are the most important accomplishments in your career so far?

Talk about big things that have happened, particularly where you were successful, and as it relates to the position you are being interviewed for. If you are just starting out in your career and don't have experience, try to tie it into volunteer work or other accomplishments.

_____

_____

_____

_____

_____

_____

_____

_____

_____

_____

_____

_____

_____

_____

_____

_____

3. Which school subject did you like most and why?

Highlight how much you enjoyed the subject and why you are passionate about it. If it relates to the job you are applying for, talk about why it is relevant and helpful for the job. It may have given you the opportunity to learn some of the things you need to do the job well.

_____

_____

_____

_____

_____

_____

_____

_____

_____

_____

_____

_____

_____

_____

_____

4. Which school subject did you like least, and why?

For this question, they are looking for you to talk about why you did not like the topic, and were still willing to do the work required to pass the class. Everyone has their strengths and weaknesses. A good answer might talk about how the class was not close to your interests, and yet how you found a way to motivate yourself to enjoy and excel at some part of it.

_____

_____

_____

_____

_____

_____

_____

_____

_____

_____

_____

_____

_____

_____

5. How did you decide on the career you are now pursuing?

They want to know how you got on the path you are on. If you choose your career because you had a mentor that was passionate and instilled that passion in you, or is there something in your history that made you choose this route. Maybe you took classes on the topic in school and really enjoyed it, and wanted to continue doing what you learned in the class.

_____

_____

_____

_____

_____

_____

_____

_____

_____

_____

_____

_____

_____

_____

6. Tell me about a time when you worked under pressure –
   how did you cope?

This could be any time where you had to multiple things at once, or had to correct an error. For a coffee shop worker, it would be wise to talk about how you handle the daily morning rush. If you are new professional in your field talk about projects, maybe you had a teacher who would assign homework last minute. You do not have to stick strictly with examples directly from the workplace. Here is the opportunity to share one of your CAR stories.

_____

_____

_____

_____

_____

_____

_____

_____

_____

_____

_____

_____

_____

_____

7. What is your biggest weakness or limitation?

For this question, most people try to make a strength that is also a weakness. For example, if you were in an interview and you said your biggest strength and weakness is that you want to help people. While this might be fine for some jobs, but not always. You may need to present a weakness and talk about how you handle it. This depends on the job and the employer. Some people want to hear the first one and others the second, so be careful. A really good way to approach this question is with a CAR story, where you started off not knowing how to do something, you learned how and then exceled at it.

_____

_____

_____

_____

_____

_____

_____

_____

_____

_____

_____

_____

8. What are your greatest strengths?

With this question make sure your strengths match the job you are interviewing for. Answers tend to be along the lines of being a hard worker, paying attention to detail, working on a team, being organized, responsible, or able to follow policies and procedures. Be prepared to illustrate how you have used these strengths with a CAR story.

_____

_____

_____

_____

_____

_____

_____

_____

_____

_____

_____

_____

_____

_____

_____

9. What is the first job you held, and what did you learn from it?

First, have you had a job before?
If you have not held a job talk about things you learned to do in school, or in a volunteer situation. Maybe you learned not to procrastinate, how to be social, or time management skills?

If you have had a job:
Talk about things you have learned, really talk about it, and remember, focus on the positive. Perhaps you were able to increase sales, attract more customers, or change things slightly to make a difference. Always make sure you have the opportunity to let the interviewer know what you contributed.

_____

_____

_____

_____

_____

_____

_____

_____

_____

_____

10. Tell me about the worst job you have ever had.

For this question be careful. Employers do not want to hear you speak badly about your previous boss, or coworkers. The best thing you can do in this situation is to share a CAR story where you turn a negative into a positive. There is always a chance to learn from every situation. You can use that to your advantage. Perhaps you were not a good fit in the job, or they were understaffed constantly, running out of products, or the company had no rules or regulations.

_____

_____

_____

_____

_____

_____

_____

_____

_____

_____

_____

_____

_____

_____

11. Why are you the best person for this job?

Talk about the knowledge, skills, and abilities that you would bring to the organization. For those entering the workforce, things like time management, attention to detail, and other skills you can learn elsewhere are important. For more experienced individuals, talk about those same knowledge skills and abilities, but be more specific, if you have knowledge of a particular system or tool the organization uses, you can talk about it. Be prepared with a CAR story, and be flexible as to which one would fit better to answer the question.

_____

_____

_____

_____

_____

_____

_____

_____

_____

_____

_____

_____

_____

12. Why should I hire you?

A good answer will again approach this from the position of the skills and experiences you possess, which are directly needed for the job you are applying for. Personality can come into play if they relate how their personality lends itself to the position being offered. For example, if they are applying to a position at a coffee shop, it is likely that they will need to be able to interact with people for several hours. They do not want to hire someone who does not like working with or being around others. It is most important to match it to how your skills and abilities would be beneficial, and make you the right person for the job.

_____

_____

_____

_____

_____

_____

_____

_____

_____

_____

_____

13. What is the minimum salary you would accept?

This question you need to do some research for before you get into the interview. This question will probably only be asked if they really like you, and probably would not happen in the first round of interviews. You should can find salary ranges online on sites like onetonline.org. While you should know what your minimum salary is, you do not want to answer this question with a number. A good answer would be something like you are looking for the experience and opportunity to grow with the company, and while salary is important, there is more that you are considering.

_____

_____

_____

_____

_____

_____

_____

_____

_____

_____

_____

14. What has been the biggest accomplishment in your life to date?

Now this question seems like they want you to open up about your personal life. BE CAREFUL! They aren't looking for you to say I ran a marathon in 4 hours (unless you are applying for sponsorship). They want to know if you were successful in your work life. For example, surpassing your sales goals for several months in a row, or completing a major project. If you are new to the workforce I would say something like the marathon because to run a marathon it takes months of training and dedication. Best place to use a CAR story to get the whole picture across.

_____

_____

_____

_____

_____

_____

_____

_____

_____

_____

_____

_____

15. What strategy do you use when you have to work with someone that you do not necessarily like?

Here is an interpersonal question, and a situation you will invariably face in real life. While it would be nice to say ignore them, you cannot always do that! They are looking for you to say something like "I would do my best to get along with them and remember that we have to work together to be successful". Use a successful and well thought out CAR story here if you have one.

_____

_____

_____

_____

_____

_____

_____

_____

_____

_____

_____

_____

_____

_____

_____

16. How would your co-workers describe you?

Stay away from the negatives. They want to know that you are willing to work as a team (which you will probably have to) and you treat other people well. Think about what positive things your coworkers would actually say about you.

_____

_____

_____

_____

_____

_____

_____

_____

_____

_____

_____

_____

_____

_____

_____

_____

_____

_____

17. Do you like working as part of a group, or on your own? Why?

This question is very much job dependent. You should always make it clear that you can work as part of a team and on your own. The person performing the interview will know what type of work you will be doing and they want to make sure that you match the position you are applying for. So answer truthfully, it saves both groups time if you don't end up not enjoying your job or they have to replace you.

_____

_____

_____

_____

_____

_____

_____

_____

_____

_____

_____

_____

_____

18. What is it about this position that interests you the most?

Be honest, unless you are just looking to make some extra cash. Everyone knows the main reason people work is for money. So stay away from answers regarding money. It's better to say you are looking for work experience, and from your research on the company, you can see yourself really being able to contribute there. Most employers understand that some jobs have a shelf-life for some employees, and that some employees would not stay in a position like working at a fast food restaurant. So, what's in it for you is a focus, however, add in what's in it for them which you will bring to the position.

_____

_____

_____

_____

_____

_____

_____

_____

_____

_____

_____

19. Why are you interested in this company?

This question is geared to see if you have done any research on an organization. As a general rule you should know what the organization does, what their mission statement is, and what the job you are applying for basically entails. If possible, go to the location, if a retail operation, go in and look around. Check out LinkedIn to see if you have any contacts there.

_____

_____

_____

_____

_____

_____

_____

_____

_____

_____

_____

_____

_____

_____

_____

20. What career changes do you see yourself making in the next five years?

This one is set up because they want to gage whether or not you are likely want to move up or out. It is always good to have some sort of plan. It does not have to be *become a CEO*; it can be something like become a supervisor at some point down the road. Mentioning that you plan to be very focused on learning the job, and excelling, and only after that would you ever thing of 'what is next'. Your focus is more on the immediate position.

_____

_____

_____

_____

_____

_____

_____

_____

_____

_____

_____

_____

_____

21.Can you give me an example of a time when you had to work under pressure?

For this question, think about the times that you have had to do something under time constraints or with certain standards you had to meet. Use your CAR story with the result that lets the interviewer know you can handle yourself in any situation.

_____

_____

_____

_____

_____

_____

_____

_____

_____

_____

_____

_____

_____

_____

_____

_____

22. What criteria (things) are most important to you in a job?

This is a very helpful question to gage whether or not you will fit into the job position, and the organization. Are you looking to mobility in the organization, a learning environment, independence to do work the way you see fit? The main point of this question is to see what you value in your job.

_____

_____

_____

_____

_____

_____

_____

_____

_____

_____

_____

_____

_____

_____

_____

23. How do you describe personal success?

This one is pretty straight forward. Since this is being asked at a job interview, do not say something like you want to sit on a beach all day relaxing. Consider that in general terms, you may want to end each day knowing you have contributed your best work, helped colleagues and customers, and maybe learned something new. Also, success may be to stay close to your family, and inspire them and enjoy your time together. This is a good question to really think about before the interview. (Also, it is a good way to live life – knowing what success looks like for you.)

_____

_____

_____

_____

_____

_____

_____

_____

_____

_____

_____

_____

24. Why are you leaving your current position – or why do you want to leave your current employer?

They are looking to see if there are any problems they should be aware of before hiring you. If you were just unhappy because of personality conflicts, or just felt like it was time to move on from that position. It's not a bad thing to say that you wanted to grow more and you could not do that at your present job.

_____

_____

_____

_____

_____

_____

_____

_____

_____

_____

_____

_____

_____

_____

_____

_____

_____

25. What did you like least about your last job?

No one wants to hear how you may not have liked where you worked or who you worked with. You may want to talk about how you were not a good fit in the organization, and why. Remember, whatever answer you give to the interviewer, they may judge you, and your situation, and consider if you would find the same thing when you had a job with them. One of the best answers to prepare before an interview.

_____

_____

_____

_____

_____

_____

_____

_____

_____

_____

_____

_____

_____

26. What did you like most about your last job?

This question is geared toward your preferences in the workplace. You can talk about how you had great coworkers or a great boss, however, they will not be coming with you to the new job, so more beneficial would be to talk about the organization and what got you excited. Maybe your team was great because you had the opportunity to learn more about different areas, or there was always some way to advance in your professional development. May be they let you have flexible work hours. The possible answers for this are endless.

_____

_____

_____

_____

_____

_____

_____

_____

_____

_____

_____

_____

_____

27. Describe what you do/did at your last job?

Being able to explain what you did/do is an excellent way of knowing how well you do your job. For some this might be easy if it is a job that requires manual tasks, but for someone who has to think a lot this can be quite difficult. Ideally you will have 4 or 5 things that are the major responsibilities in your job, and you can briefly explain them.

_____

_____

_____

_____

_____

_____

_____

_____

_____

_____

_____

_____

_____

_____

_____

_____

28. Describe a time when you had to supervise a difficult person.

This question is geared toward a management position. So not everyone will be asked this question. They want to know that you will follow company policy and do what is appropriate in a stressful situation. They want to know how you were able to appropriately work through a disciplinary situation, if that is what it took to get the person back 'on-side'. Perfect opportunity for a CAR story.

_____

_____

_____

_____

_____

_____

_____

_____

_____

_____

_____

_____

_____

_____

_____

29. Why do you think you will like working in this position?

This question is a 'crystal ball' question, as nobody would know unless they have been working in the job. This is a way to test what you think the job will be, and how you line up with the duties. Based on your knowledge of what this job is, select the things you can get excited about and talk about them.

_____

_____

_____

_____

_____

_____

_____

_____

_____

_____

_____

_____

_____

_____

_____

_____

30. Describe a situation in which you were able to use persuasion to successfully convince someone to see things your way.

This question is important. Persuasion is an important of many jobs, whether it is buying the weekly special, or helping someone select the best option for them, and maybe up-selling them. Persuasion is also important in dealing with your coworkers and possibly your bosses, if an important change needs to occur. So really think about this question when you a preparing for an interview. If you have an example from work that is excellent maybe you persuaded your boss to let you try a new sales technique and your team was able to finally reach its sales goal for that week, this would be the CAR story to tell.

_____

_____

_____

_____

_____

_____

_____

_____

_____

_____

31. Tell me about a time when you had to deal with a very stressful situation.

This is a behavioral question. They want to know if you are capable of handling yourself in stress. This would be an excellent time to use that CARs answer. Talk about how you handled several things at once, or how something went wrong and you had to correct it. Maybe you had some help from fellow coworkers or you were able to manage your time successfully.

_____

_____

_____

_____

_____

_____

_____

_____

_____

_____

_____

_____

_____

_____

32. Describe a time when you went against company policy – why did you do it, and how did it turn out?

The key take away is you do not ever want to go against company policy. If it's minor, you might get a reprimand but if it's a big mistake you might get fired. They want to know that you learned that it is best to follow company policy. This being said you should never go along with a policy that breaks the law.

_____

_____

_____

_____

_____

_____

_____

_____

_____

_____

_____

_____

_____

_____

_____

33. Describe the biggest project you have worked on – how were you involved?

They want to know if you have ever worked on long term projects, and what your role was in it. Did you make action possible, help others get work done, or help develop the central project? If you are freshly done with your degree, and have little work experience you can always talk about a school experience with a project. Have a few CAR stories that you could respond with.

_____

_____

_____

_____

_____

_____

_____

_____

_____

_____

_____

_____

_____

34. Describe the most creative solution you have had to a problem.

This question is gauging your ability to problem solve. Some problems require new ideas. Even if you were not able to use your idea, it is ok to tell them what your idea was and how it would have changed the situation. If you have a real experience, use the CAR story format and make sure you take the credit you deserve.

_____

_____

_____

_____

_____

_____

_____

_____

_____

_____

_____

_____

_____

_____

35. What is the toughest group you have had to lead? What were the obstacles and how did you handle them?

This question is for anyone applying to a management position. If you get asked this question you will want to use the CARs method again. Maybe it was solved by following the company policy, or again you can always refer back to something you learned in school.

_____

_____

_____

_____

_____

_____

_____

_____

_____

_____

_____

_____

_____

_____

_____

_____

_____

_____

36. What is the best decision you have ever made – how did you know it was a good decision?

This is a tough one. Keep it relevant to your work or school experience. It may be the best decision based on a sale, a new client, a completed project, a happy customer, looking at something in a new way and making a change, it could be hiring someone, and so forth. A great question to have more than one answer to.

_____

_____

_____

_____

_____

_____

_____

_____

_____

_____

_____

_____

_____

_____

_____

37. What is your greatest sales related achievement to date?

This question may be relevant if you are applying in a sales position or looking to become a manager in a sales department. This one is pretty straight forward, use the CARS method to talk about the challenge, how you dealt with it and what the results were.

_____

_____

_____

_____

_____

_____

_____

_____

_____

_____

_____

_____

_____

_____

_____

_____

38. Describe the best presentation you have ever made –
what made it so good?

This is a skill that many employers would like you to have, even if it is presenting to a few people in your group, not necessarily a large audience. This question is probably not geared to working in the fast food industry and is more likely to be seen in the consulting, or professional world. A good presentation is made up of several factors, be sure that you can include at least these main ideas: Were you able to get the main points across? Include in your CAR story: Were you able to engage the audience? Did your presentation make sense for your audience? Make sure you talk about why it was so good, and the feedback you received.

_____

_____

_____

_____

_____

_____

_____

_____

_____

_____

_____

39. Describe a time when you did not agree with your supervisor – how did you handle the situation?

This is a difficult situation for anyone to be in. Talk about what the disagreement was and what happened. Often times the supervisor has more information than you do, and you cannot always see the full picture. If you had a disagreement talk about what happened and how you handled the situation afterwards. They want to know that you respect your boss and your coworkers.

_____

_____

_____

_____

_____

_____

_____

_____

_____

_____

_____

_____

_____

_____

40. Describe a time when you were particularly creative or resourceful.

This is another situational question. They want know if there was a time you did not have the resources to do what you were required to do. Use the CARs method for answering this question. If you cannot think of a work situation, it is okay to use a personal example, maybe your car broke down and you had to get somewhere important.

_____

_____

_____

_____

_____

_____

_____

_____

_____

_____

_____

_____

_____

_____

41. What are your weaknesses and limitations?

This question is asked to find out how self-aware you are. Do you know what you are not able to do? How do you describe it? What are you doing to overcome it? This is not where you give a weakness that will prevent you from being considered for the position, it is a time to respond with something that is rather minor as a duty of the job, and something you are willing to learn.

_____

_____

_____

_____

_____

_____

_____

_____

_____

_____

_____

_____

_____

_____

_____

42. How do you manage your time?

Questions about time, in general are often asked in interviews. The interviewer may ask you how many times you have been late for work in a set period of time. They are looking to see if you value and respect time. Are you able to set priorities, and work to deadlines? Some people manage time by due dates or task importance, some have daily to do lists. Time management can be daily, hourly, very specific or general.

_____

_____

_____

_____

_____

_____

_____

_____

_____

_____

_____

_____

_____

_____

43. Describe your idea of a perfect supervisor.

When you respond to this question it is okay to say you want a supervisor that will not micromanage you, is willing to train you, or be supportive and provide assistance.

_____

_____

_____

_____

_____

_____

_____

_____

_____

_____

_____

_____

_____

_____

_____

_____

_____

_____

44. Describe a time when you took a risk.

This question can be a double edged sword. Do not talk about something that would make you seem like possible trouble for the organization. Don't share a story that could be perceived as you not being someone who generally follows the rules, policies and procedures. Never take a safety risk, or put the company or your team members at risk. If you have a work related experience talk about that experience using the CAR format. It is okay to admit you failed, but make sure that you talk about how you learned from the experience.

_____

_____

_____

_____

_____

_____

_____

_____

_____

_____

_____

_____

_____

45. What three words describe you best?

This question is a tough one, three words is never enough to describe who you are. Think about who you would be in the job and what parts of you fit the work that you would be doing. Let's look at a coffee shop worker for example, they would probably want to hire someone who described themselves as friendly, coffee-lover, and detail oriented. Friendly, because I would want someone to be able to constantly interact with people. Coffee-lover because I would want someone who has an interest in the product I sell and may stay longer because they have passion for the product. Lastly detail-oriented because I do not want them wasting product by not facilitating the right order getting to the customer.

_____

_____

_____

_____

_____

_____

_____

_____

_____

_____

_____

46. In what areas of your present job are you the strongest?

Think about the things that you have been told you have done well. Be sure to relate them back to the job you are applying for. Write CAR stories for each strength so you can say why you have said it is a strength if you are asked to elaborate.

_____

_____

_____

_____

_____

_____

_____

_____

_____

_____

_____

_____

_____

_____

_____

_____

_____

_____

47. Describe a situation where others you were working with disagreed with your ideas. What did you do?

This question is asking you to talk about how you manage conflict. You should be truthful did you take it poorly or well. Talk about how and why you responded and the details of what happened. For example, I was working with my team and we had an issue with a particular aspect of the project. We discussed the issue and one of the team thought my idea was not practical. I responded by asking them why and we discussed the issue from there.

_____

_____

_____

_____

_____

_____

_____

_____

_____

_____

_____

_____

48. How do you deal with politics and gossip in the workplace?

Employers are well aware of their responsibility to have a respectful workplace. They look for employees who do not cause drama. You may be able to describe a situation where you have refused to gossip, or requested that someone not tell you something that they were not willing to talk to the person themselves about. Obviously the best answer is that you stay clear of talking about other people.

_____

_____

_____

_____

_____

_____

_____

_____

_____

_____

_____

_____

_____

_____

49. Describe the biggest mistake you have made at work.

Be honest, talk through the situation using a CAR story. Be sure to not give the absolute worst mistake you have ever made, look for one that is not over the top, and could be judged by the interviewer as making you a risk to hire.

_____

_____

_____

_____

_____

_____

_____

_____

_____

_____

_____

_____

_____

_____

_____

_____

50. Describe a time when your integrity/honesty was challenged. How did you handle it?

This is another situation for a CAR story if you do have this situation in your past. It is ok if you have never had your honesty challenged!

_____

_____

_____

_____

_____

_____

_____

_____

_____

_____

_____

_____

_____

_____

_____

_____

_____

_____

_____

51. Describe a time when you saw a potential problem as an opportunity. What did you do and how did it work out?

This is an opportunity to show that you can look at situations critically. They also want to know if you can take a possibly negative situation and adjust it before something happens. For example, someone left a large puddle of water on the lunch room floor and it was definitely in the pathway of employees. It would be good to know that you cleaned up the spill before it became a problem. For someone in a different work setting, it might be identifying a flaw in a system, a customer service issue that could be corrected, or a timeline that was not going to be met.

_____

_____

_____

_____

_____

_____

_____

_____

_____

_____

_____

_____

52. What hours do you like to work?

This question is very important in determining if you will be able to work the hours they need you to work. You should always be willing to work if you are able to work, however, it is okay to say that you are unavailable at times. Most employers understand that.

_____

_____

_____

_____

_____

_____

_____

_____

_____

_____

_____

_____

_____

_____

_____

_____

_____

53. What REALLY upsets you?

This question may be asked in a number of different ways, using word like upset or angry. Tell them the truth, and be careful to make sure that you being upset would make sense to most people. The best middle ground for this question would be to talk about the things that frustrate you, like someone not being thoughtful, or going out of their way to be difficult.

_____

_____

_____

_____

_____

_____

_____

_____

_____

_____

_____

_____

_____

_____

54. What motivates you?

This question is again where they don't want you to say money. Everyone is motivated by money to some extent. So think about things similar to having a great team, or knowing that you are helping others. These will not work in every situation so think carefully when you are asked this question, and have a CAR story prepared.

_____

_____

_____

_____

_____

_____

_____

_____

_____

_____

_____

_____

_____

_____

_____

_____

_____

55. What kind of people do you most like to work with?

This question is looking at your fit in the company. Be honest are you the person who likes to work with people who get along well with others, or do you prefer to work where you are working with people who also like to work alone. There are many different aspects to people you could be working with, so think carefully about who you would like to work with.

_____

_____

_____

_____

_____

_____

_____

_____

_____

_____

_____

_____

_____

_____

56. Describe a time when you had to make a decision without all the information you needed. How did you handle it?

They want to know that you are willing to do research or ask for help from your coworkers and supervisors. If you do not know what to do, did you check the manual, or is this a new problem? It would be good to have a CAR story that discusses a new problem you experienced, and possibly helped solve.

_____

_____

_____

_____

_____

_____

_____

_____

_____

_____

_____

_____

_____

_____

57. Describe a time when you had an upset customer or client and how you made things right. What thought process did you go through? What was the outcome?

This is a very common interview question. It is often used to find out how you will handle conflict or if you are able to stand your ground. Use the CARs method to talk about what happened, how you handled the upset person and what were the outcomes for you and the customer.

_____

_____

_____

_____

_____

_____

_____

_____

_____

_____

_____

_____

_____

_____

58. How do you make complicated ideas simple?

This question may be geared toward more professional jobs. It is important for people working in a professional environment to be able to explain something that is complicated in terms that a non-expert can understand. For example, we know that houses are insulated, most people do not need to know the whole process and all the detail of how to insulate a house, however, they may need to understand the basics. Think of the job you are being interviewed for, and any area the interviewer may ask you to explain your understanding of a particular part. Also, you may have a way of understanding something generally considered complicated, by using a system you have learned.

_____

_____

_____

_____

_____

_____

_____

_____

_____

_____

_____

59. Do you create systems for organizing your day?

The interviewer is looking to see if you are a person who plans things out in advance of your day. Do you write lists? Do you have goals? How do you make sure you do the things you had planned to, or are supposed to do each day? A CAR story is a good way to show you are organized.

_____

_____

_____

_____

_____

_____

_____

_____

_____

_____

_____

_____

_____

_____

_____

_____

60. Describe how you would handle a situation if you were required to finish multiple tasks by the end of the day, and there was no conceivable way that you could finish them.

This is not a situation where they want to hear that you shift the blame to someone else. It is important that you handle the question in a way that shows you would be responsible. You may give an early alert to your supervisor so they could help you make priorities, or have them assign someone to help you out. If you have been in this situation, use a CAR story to describe it. You may want to discuss how to correct this in the future.

_____

_____

_____

_____

_____

_____

_____

_____

_____

_____

_____

61. Describe a time when you have brought an innovative idea to work. Was the change made? Why or why not?

Sometimes innovative ideas are dismissed due to company policies, current or past practices, or the desire to not have to interrupt something that seems to be working fine. If you have ever given your ideas to a supervisor talk about what happened. Did they like it or did your idea get turned down? If it did, why? Maybe it was the wrong timing, cost too much money, or you needed support from other people who were not able to help.

_____

_____

_____

_____

_____

_____

_____

_____

_____

_____

_____

_____

62. Give me an example of a time when you had to conform to a policy even though you did not agree with it.

This can be another tricky question to answer as they are looking to find out if you will be willing and able to do something that you may not have agreed with. Sometimes you will have to turn people away and tell them you aren't able to assist them, and it would seem like it made sense to help them out.   Think of privacy information in a government setting, where there are reasons for not giving out certain information. It is risky for the employer to have you doing things that are outside your job scope, as you may believe that breaking the rules are not a big deal.

_____

_____

_____

_____

_____

_____

_____

_____

_____

_____

63. Can you tell me about a time when you persuaded others to accept your idea?

This is a question that would be used in a professional setting to find out how good you are at persuading someone. There are many possible reasons to persuade someone to do something. You should always try to come across as respectful and courteous. Talk about how the changes were important to the organization. Did you use facts to help persuade them? What methods did you use? Talk about the importance of why you felt it necessary to persuade them using a CAR story.

_____

_____

_____

_____

_____

_____

_____

_____

_____

_____

_____

_____

64. Can you give me an example of your resourcefulness?

This question again can be very bad for your interview, if you answer it the wrong way. It can also be very good. Do not say that you were resourceful at stealing stuff from your office or you used your abilities to do something that could be seen as wrong. You should always talk about how you did something that was a benefit to your team.

_____

_____

_____

_____

_____

_____

_____

_____

_____

_____

_____

_____

_____

_____

_____

_____

65. Describe the most significant written document, report or presentation you have completed.

This question is a question on what you see as your best work, so make sure you give them your best work. When interviewing for a position where report writing or presentations are a focus of the position, it is a good idea to bring along a writing sample. You do not have to leave the document with the interviewer, they will likely take a quick look and return it to you. Make sure to summarize the (positive) feedback you received.

_____

_____

_____

_____

_____

_____

_____

_____

_____

_____

_____

_____

_____

66. What have you done to improve your knowledge in the last year?

When answering this question think about how your knowledge would make you more valuable in the job. Did you study customer relations, read about marketing, join a business book club? If you have done nothing at all to make yourself more valuable in the workplace, perhaps you should think about getting a book, or downloading a book, and starting to read it and put into practice, something that makes you more valuable as an employee.

_____

_____

_____

_____

_____

_____

_____

_____

_____

_____

_____

_____

Part IV – Questions to Ask the Interviewer

The following questions are examples of appropriate questions to ask. Prepare 3-5 questions and likely 3 questions will be enough. You will be able to tell if they sincerely want you to ask more questions after about the 3rd one.

- What new products will you be introducing in the future?
- How has the economy affected your business?
- What is your supervision style?
- What do you like most about working here?
- What is the next step in the process?
- What is the purpose of the job?
- What key outcomes or results are expected?
- What percentage of time would be spent (with customers, on the phone, traveling, using the computer, researching, *etc.?*)
- What qualities are you looking for in the person who will do this job?
- What do you expect to see accomplished in the next year?
- What type of orientation do you give to new employees?
- What kinds of resources are available to do this job?
- What are some of the biggest challenges that someone in this positions would face?
- Is there anything else you would like to know about me?

Your list of questions you would like to ask:

1. _____

_____

_____

_____

_____

_____

2. _____

_____

_____

_____

_____

_____

3. _____

_____

_____

_____

_____

_____

4. _____

_____

_____

_____

_____

_____

5. _____

_____

_____

_____

_____

_____

Part V – Conclusion

Think about the close of the interview – how do you want to be remembered?

Write out the final thoughts you would like to leave as a last impression.

(You want them to know that you are interested in the job – you have the required skills and strengths to contribute – a mutually beneficial relationship).

Your Closing Statement:

_____

_____

_____

_____

_____

_____

_____

_____

_____

_____

_____

_____

_____

Before you leave the interview, be sure to let the interviewer know that you are interested in the position, of course providing that you *are* interested in the position, now you have more information about it.

It is acceptable to ask what the next steps are. They may have more applicants to interview, they may want to do a second interview with the top applicants. Each company will have different hiring policies.

It is not a good idea to ask if you got the job, or how you did in the interview. If the interviewer is so impressed with you, they may decide to make an offer on the spot, however it is for them to mention, not for you to ask.

Leave the room with a firm handshake, eye contact and a smile!

Part V – After the Interview

After your interview take time to think about how you did in the interview.

Did you successfully represent yourself? Did you prepare enough? Did you do a good job of telling your CAR stories? Would you do anything differently? Were there any questions you could not answer?

_____

_____

_____

_____

_____

What did you learn about yourself?

_____

_____

_____

_____

Immediately after the interview you can write a thank you note, or send a thank you email to the interviewer. It is ok to lightly mention a few of your strengths for the job, thank them for their time, and say you are looking forward to hearing further from them.

Interview Do's & Don'ts

Do:

- Answer only direct questions – clarify if required
- Handshake warmly and make eye contact
- Prepare answers to common questions
- Take extra copies of your resume
- Take a listing of your references
- Ask intelligent questions
- Research the organization
- Take only what you need
- Think before you speak
- Know the exact location
- Arrive 10 minutes early
- Bring paper and a pen
- Listen attentively
- Dress properly
- Smile
- Answer questions fully
- Prepare to ask questions
- Use recent CAR stories for examples
- Remember the interviewer's name
- Follow-up if you agreed to provide the interviewer with something
- Ask what is next in the hiring cycle
- Summarize key requirements and link your attributes to them
- Be positive
- Send a thank you note
- Be precise
- Allow the interviewer to set the tone

Don't:

- Sit before being invited to sit
- Interrupt the interviewer
- Initiate a discussion about money or benefits
- Badmouth past employer or supervisor
- Lie
- Fidget or slouch in your chair
- Shout or whisper
- Stare
- Lack energy
- Be too aggressive
- Make excuses
- Be in a rush to leave the room
- Talk down to the interviewer
- Get into an argument
- Point out an interviewers' mistake
- Eat a spicy meal or drink before the interview
- Use too much perfume or cologne
- Avoid answering any questions
- Play with a pen
- Dwell on negatives
- Wear tinted glasses
- Check your watch repeatedly
- Shuffle papers
- Use slang expressions
- Make nervous gestures such as tapping your feet, repeated clearing your throat, etc.
- Lean in too closely to the interviewer
- Sit with your arms crossed
- Play with your hair, fingernails or fidget

Once you have filled out the questions in this book and taken the time to practice out loud, and done a recording of yourself answering the questions. When you watch the video check to see if there are any nervous habits you need to eliminate. Once you feel comfortable and see yourself as being prepared, you are well on the way to interview success.

Make sure you double check the date and time of your interview a few days before. Decide what you will wear, and try it on to be sure it still fits and is in good condition. If the interview is early in the morning be sure to set an alarm or two so you wake up in plenty of time.

Print out the CAR stories and place them in a portfolio with a few extra copies of your resume and references.

If possible, do a practice run to the interview location, and if not, leave plenty of time on the day of the interview, in case you run into traffic, etc. Be sure you know the route, and write down the address and the name of the interviewers. Take the phone contact information, just in case you have an emergency and need to get a hold of them.

There is nothing better than arriving early to an interview, and having the time to compose yourself. You can do deep breathing and focus on the positive aspect of having been selected for an interview.

Be sure you are pleasant to everyone, especially in the parking lot if you are driving. Be aware as you enter the building, keeping a pleasant attitude as you find out where you are to meet the interviewer. Your interview starts as soon as you are on the premises, and you never know who is watching you as you make your way to the interview.

Best wishes on a successful job search!

9 781988 317038